THE GAME OF LIFE

Swami Tejomayananda

D1075915

CENTRAL CHINMAYA MISSION TRUST

Print up to March 2007   42,000 copies
Revised Edited Print Aug 2009 - 3000 copies
Reprint Apr 2010 - 3000 copies

Published by:
CENTRAL CHINMAYA MISSION TRUST
Sandeepany Sadhanalaya
Mumbai – 400 072. INDIA

Tel: 91-22-28572367 • Fax: 91-22-28573065
Email: ccmtpublications@chinmayamission.com
Website: www.chinmayamission.com

Distribution Centre in USA:
CHINMAYA MISSION WEST
Publications Division,
560 Bridgetown Pike,
Langhorne, PA 19053, USA.

Tel: (215) 396-0390 • Fax: (215) 396-9710
Email: publications@chinmaya.org
Website: www.chinmayapublications.org

Printed by: Thomson Press
Thane Belapur Road, Airoli
Navi Mumbai 400 078, India

Price: 35/-

ISBN: 978-81-7597-141-7

CONTENTS

PREFACE

"When you are hungry you have to eat. No other person, not even your best friend can eat for you. Yes, they may eat but your hunger will not be satisfied". Pujya Swami Tejomayanandaji's talks on "The Game of Life" for the children attending Bala Vihar camp took off with these simple and obvious words. Over the next five days he went on to unfold the intricacies of the game of life and give clues and practical tips on how to play it and come out a winner. In an easy-to-understand language for children and adults alike, he answered basic questions like, what is life, what is its purpose, what are the rules that govern it and how to tune the mind.

As this particular 'game' is being played by all, we thought of bringing home to you some notes on the talks given by Pujya Guruji.

We thank all those who helped in the original and previous editions of this book. This new edition is illustrated with cartoons by Brni. Nivedita Chaitanya, Melbourne, in her own unique style. We acknowledge the help rendered by Smt Tripta Bhalla, Mumbai. May Pujya Gurudev's blessing be on all.

Publishers

ᏀAME TIME

Everyone, especially children love two things the most – listening to story and playing games. Now we are going to play the game of life.

When we feel hungry we have to eat. No other person can eat for us. When we are sick, if somebody else takes the medicine, it is of no use to us. In the same way, we have to live our own life. Others can only help. They may teach us, but we have to learn for ourselves. In life, every person has to live their own life. Once this is understood, we realize that to make our life cheerful and happy or miserable and weepy – both is in our hands. We have the choice.

You will all agree that we must make our life beautiful and full of laughter. That is why we must make our life a game to be played.

Some people say – 'life is a dream'. To some 'life is a tragedy' or 'life is of no use'. We sometimes think something as useless and throw it away as waste. In a train some children threw away chocolate wrappers. Some Japanese children were in the same train. They picked up the wrappers and made beautiful dolls out of them. They sold them and made money! So what we make of our life is in our own hands.

Two boys were given Rs.500.00 each by their father and asked to fill the whole house with whatever they could buy with the money. They were given two days to complete the task. When he came to see, one had filled his house with garbage, the other had bought enough lamps and filled every nook and corner with light. So we have to make our choice intelligently.

To understand how to play the game of life intelligently, we will first see what is a game, what is life and then come to the actual play.

*W*HY PLAY?

What is a game?

A game is something we do for fun. A team game is played between two teams. When two parties are fighting, it is a war. In the game, we may oppose but still friendship remains and there is peace. Whereas at the end of a war there is hatred and destruction.

Why do we play?

1. The game is played just for fun. To enjoy. No other inducement is required. No mother needs to bribe the child with chocolates to make him play. Mothers may send children out to play for their health or for their own peace of mind but children do not play games for good health. That comes automatically.

2. Professional players play for money. It is their source of livelihood.

3. The game is played for individual victory. The player plays his own game to show his own capabilities and to earn fame.

4. Games are also played to benefit society or for some social cause.

5. Some initially play for their school, then for their college, then at the national level and even international level. In victory, they bring glory to their institution or country.

Thus, games can be played for fun, for money, for individual fame, as service to the people or for national glory. When the game is played for the nation, the individual enjoys, gets name, fame and money and at the same time brings glory to the nation. When an individual plays the same game only for money, he may get his money but nothing great is achieved. In playing for the higher purpose, the lower ones are always gained. Why not maximize the achievement and play for the higher purpose? When we play, sometimes we lose, sometimes we win. When we lose, there is no anger, hatred or jealousy. The captain of the losing team goes and congratulates the opposing team. That is sportsmanship.

4

Now... What is life?

Breathing is a sign of life. But life is not mere breathing or moving about or responding. Life is a series of experiences. If I say I had an experience, the question will be—experience of what? So, for an experience there must be two things. The experiencer and the object of experience – the things and beings of the world.

In the world there is the sun, the moon, the stars, ocean, planets, trees, animals, insects and people. In life, the game goes on between two parties, me and the world. If you make life a war, it will be your fight against the whole world. **Don't make life a war and fight it, make life a game and play it.**

What is the purpose of life?

1. Some people say, "Eat, drink and be merry"—that is the purpose of life. Sounds wonderful but supposing there is nothing to eat and drink...then? Or the food may be there but if the stomach is upset...then? Or if whilst eating you come to know that you have failed in your exams! Then do you enjoy? To enjoy a simple thing like food, so many factors are necessary. So a person cannot be happy all the time. He is sometimes happy and sometimes unhappy.

2. For some people the purpose of life is to earn money. What will we do with all the accumulated money? Yes, money is required in life, but life is not meant for making money alone.

3. The game of life is played for winning. But think—can we win in any game all the time? When success becomes all important, people start cheating. Duryodhana won the game of dice against Yudhiṣṭhira by cheating. Some people

consider that when they get whatever they want, that is success. But what we get by foul means is false success. It is not true success. After kidnapping Sītādevī, Rāvaṇa was taking her to Laṅkā. Jatāyu tried to prevent him. Rāvaṇa succeeded and Jatāyu failed. But who is praised? Jatāyu, of course. Every kind of winning is not true success. In the game of life, living must be truthful and it should be for a noble goal. It is better sometimes if we fail while doing some noble work than to succeed in an ignoble deed.

The game of life can be played for pleasure, for money, for winning but what is the higher purpose? The higher purpose can be to bring glory to the nation or to serve the people. When we work for the nation, we will get enjoyment, but if we work just for money, it is not necessary that there is benefit to the nation. So the intelligent way of doing something is when maximum benefit is derived both to the nation and to the individual.

ℝULES OF THE GAME

Rules of the game

In every game that we play, there are rules. In life also we have rules for everything. There are rules for walking on the road, getting down from a bus, traffic rules, and rules for music, dancing and even in science. These rules or laws are made so that life goes on smoothly, for the safety and convenience of all and for harmonious living amongst people. **The rules by which we play the game of life are called dharma.**

If we do not follow the traffic rules, there will be accidents. Singing or playing instruments without following music rules (tāla etc.) will only create noise. For keeping our body healthy, there are rules for eating, sleeping, exercise and bathing. It is our duty to keep the body healthy. So the rules for keeping a healthy body are called dharma of the body.

If dharma is obeyed, then there will be no problems. Dharma is of two types – do's and don'ts. Do's are to be followed and don'ts are to be avoided. For example, when we follow the dharma or laws of electricity it becomes a blessing. When disobeyed (don't touch a live wire!), it will be dangerous. The do's and don'ts when followed, bring peace and fearlessness and when disobeyed, cause agitation.

Now for every game there are some general rules and some specific rules. The general rule is that all must play by fair means and must accept the decision of the referee. Each game, like football or cricket, will have its own specific rules. Each person must follow the rules and play his role as well as he can. The goalkeeper in football must prevent the other team from making goals.

In life also there is a general dharma which is applicable to all irrespective of age, position or nationality. One is that all people must perform their duty. Suppose the cooks in the āśrama go on a strike, we will not get food. If people do not perform their duty everything will be disrupted. Another general dharma is that all must be truthful.

What is our particular dharma? Wherever we are, whether in the āśrama, home or school or travelling in a train, we are told what to do and what is our responsibility. For our health we must bathe daily. This is the general dharma (सामान्य धर्म). Now, if we get pneumonia, we must not bathe. This is the particular dharma (विशेष धर्म) prompted by particular circumstances. So all must follow dharma.

What is the purpose of dharma?

The following Vaidika prayer illustrates this very clearly:

ॐ भद्रं कर्णेभिः श्रृणुयाम देवा:
भद्रं पश्येमाक्षभिर्यजत्रा:।
स्थिरैरङ्गैस्तुष्टुवाग्ं सस्तनूभि
व्यशेम देवहितं यदायु:॥

om bhadraṁ karṇebhiḥ śṛṇuyāma devāḥ

bhadraṁ paśyemā-kṣabhir-yajatrāḥ,

sthirairaṅgaistuṣṭuvāgṁ sastanūbhiḥ

vyaśema devahitaṁ yadāyuḥ.

Om is the common name of the Lord. Rāma or Kṛṣṇa are His particular names.

ॐ भद्रं कर्णेभि: श्रृणुयाम देवा: bhadraṁ karṇebhiḥ śṛṇuyāma devāḥ

With our ears, may we hear what is good or what is auspicious. To hear good, everyone must speak good. I too must speak good as I hear my own words before others hear me. Everyone says the prayer together, may we hear good and good means truth. We must all speak the truth, so we all will hear the truth.

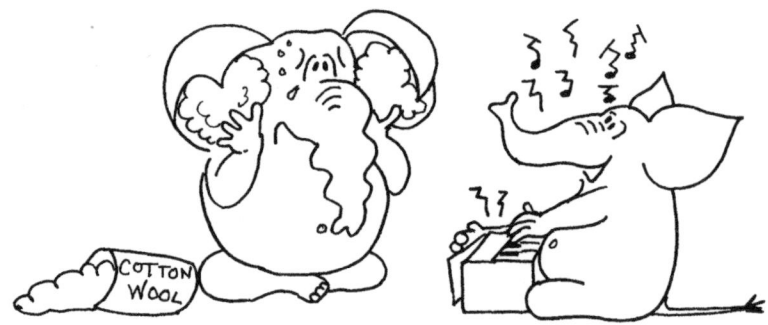

भद्रं पश्येमाक्षभिर्यजत्रा:

bhadraṁ paśyemā-kṣabhir-yajatrāḥ

May our eyes see auspicious, noble and beautiful things. So we must make everything beautiful and auspicious around us. We must keep everything clean.

स्थिरैरङ्गैस्तुष्टुवाग्ं सस्तनूभि

sthirairaṅgaistuṣṭuvāgṁ sastanūbhiḥ

O Lord! May we have firm limbs to serve others. May we be healthy and strong, then alone can we serve others.

व्यशेम देवहितं यदायु:॥ vyaśema devahitaṁ yadāyuḥ

May we live our allotted life-span in doing good. We do not ask for one day more to live nor to die a day earlier. May we live our life singing Your glory, seeing and hearing auspiciousness all around us. Have you seen the famous three monkeys? They depict 'See no evil, hear no evil, speak no evil'. The above prayer gives the positive side of this. See good, hear good, speak good.

So far we have seen the following:

a. The rules of the game of life are called dharma.

b. There are general rules and also specific rules.

c. Also dharma is of two types. Do's and don'ts.

d. Following dharma makes us happy. Doing adharma makes us unhappy. If we do what should not be done, we become fearful. If we do not do what should be done there is agitation. We therefore pray to God, "May there be happiness and auspiciousness all around; i.e. may all follow dharma and be happy.

PRAY AND PLAY

Why should we pray?

First of all why should we analyze so much? Before hoisting a flag, we fix a pole in the ground. Then we shake it to see if it is firm. The understanding that we gain by analysis makes our knowledge firm. Otherwise, when we are saying our prayers and someone says there is no use of praying, we will become doubtful and get shaken.

Why should we pray? Why not just be good and do good work? For any good work, we require the strength and a noble goal or an ideal. Do we have the strength to be good and to do good always? For a person, who is doing good, the question arises why should I go on doing good when others are not doing so? Besides, all the time we are not able to do good. That requires tremendous strength. In order to avoid getting shaken from doing good, we must become strong. So we must understand the strength of prayer. For a fan to rotate, it must be connected to the electric supply. We can call the connection, the fan's prayer to the source of power. The Lord is the source of all goodness. The strength we require to lead a noble life is called spiritual strength (ādhyātmika śakti) and God is the ultimate source of all strength. He gives us the strength to do good.

Prayer is not begging – give me this, give me that. We want to do good but every time our mind is such that it gets distracted. Duryodhana also knew what was good and what was bad but his mind was such that all the time he went on doing only the wrong things. So, we pray for strength.

Why should we pray to God?

We should pray to God so that our mind gets tuned to Him and all His qualities and powers will come to us. We should also pray in order to please Him. In life, as we do our dharma we must remember God.

When people do good work for the sake of money and if they don't get it, they stop. When we work for Bhagavān, even if people criticize or crucify us, we will not be shaken.

Also in prayer we remember that beauty, strength, talent, everything is a blessing and gift of the Lord. Then we will not become proud and arrogant. Rāvaṇa suffered a lot, but he did not surrender to God because of his ego. Prayer helps us to remove our ego. So, now we understand that when we pray, we derive spiritual strength, we dedicate our work to God and also we remove our ego.

Who or what is God? Is there one God or many? Is He real or just imaginary?

God is one. His powers are manifold! How is that? See, you are one but also many! When you are listening you are the hearer, when seeing, the seer; when singing, the singer; when joking, the joker! The seer, hearer, singer are not different, you are only one. You are the hearer when you are using the power of hearing in you, the seer whilst using the power of seeing in you. The power is one but the instruments through which it manifests are the ears or the eyes. The power is in you, it cannot remain separate from you. In the same way, understand, **God is one. He is one with you. His power is one but its expression is manifold.**

Now when you make a pot, you are called the pot-maker, when you break it, the pot-breaker and when you keep it, its keeper. God is the Creator of the entire world, its Maintainer and Destroyer. Destruction means that the world becomes unmanifest. Even when the mud pot is destroyed, the mud remains. Brahmā (Creator), Viṣṇu (Sustainer) and Maheśa (Destroyer) are the expressions of the Supreme God. God is the wielder of the cosmic energy that manifests differently. The President is one and the ministers who execute his power are many. God is one. Through many ministers (devatäs) like Vāyu, Agni, Indra and Varuṇa, He governs the different powers in nature.

God is that Consciousness which enlivens the inert. Because of Him, the eyes see and the ears hear. Some people say, "There is no God". But they do not know the power because of which they are able to say those words is God. The Vedās say: *ekaṁ sat viprā bahudhā vadanti* God is one, the wise people call Him by various names.

Pray to God because He is great and through Him we get the power to be good and do good; i.e. follow our dharma.

*G*ENERAL AND SPECIFIC RULES

What are the fundamental principles of dharma?

1. Reverence for life

Everyone wants to live, no one wants to die, not even a little insect. Hence our dharma is to protect life and do all that is necessary for its sustenance. God can create, sustain and destroy life. We can only sustain and destroy, we cannot create life. So we should do all that we can to sustain our own and others lives. We should not destroy life out of fear, hatred or greed. We should not unnecessarily kill. Doing good work like pūjā (ritualistic worship) and then killing some living thing is not dharma. That is like a rākṣasa (demon). The greatest dharma is compassion towards living beings.

2. *Respect for knowledge*

No one likes to be fooled. Anyone can fool or exploit another person, when he is ignorant of something. But he forgets that he too is ignorant about certain things. When people realize that they have been fooled they don't like it. Instead of playing this foolish game of cheating others, we must have respect for knowledge and impart knowledge to others. The more you give knowledge, the more it will grow. That is why our scriptures say:

तमसो मा ज्योतिर्गमय

tamaso mā jyotir gamaya

Lead me from ignorance to knowledge.

When we give food to the hungry, his hunger is satisfied temporarily, but when you give knowledge, it is forever.

2. *Respect for happiness*

Everyone wants to live and live happily. We have no right to destroy the happiness of others. A thief was crying when another thief came to his house and stole all his things. His mother reminded him that when he stole, others must be feeling equally unhappy. From that day, he gave up stealing. Our dharma is to give happiness. It does not cost us anything to smile. If by smiling we can make others happy, why keep the smile a mile away?

4. *Integration*

Dharma is that which integrates, that which brings everyone together. To create enmity and quarrel among people is adharma. We must try to establish friendship, even if someone is speaking ill of us or of another. We are doing wrong if we break up friendships. We must bring unity despite diversity.

5. *Love*

We may think that to respect life and knowledge, bring happiness and integration are difficult things to do. Instead of doing so many things isn't there just one thing? The answer is 'yes'. It is love. Where there is love, the above four happen. For example, parents love their children. They feed and clothe them and see to it that no harm comes to them. They send them to school to get knowledge. They do all they can to make them happy and always attempt to keep the family united. In love, sustenance of life, respect for knowledge, giving joy and being united – all happens. It is a four-in-one dharma.

The test of love is that we are concerned about the happiness of the loved ones and are always ready to serve them. **Love is the essence of dharma**. If there is no love, everything else loses its value. Love for God is called bhakti. So a ritual (pūjā) done without love will be of no use. If love is present, there is happiness in life.

What is our particular dharma?

Now as youngsters what is our particular dharma?

मातृदेवो भव mātṛ devo bhava:

Regard mother as God.

A mother's divine qualities are derived from God. She is the nourisher and provider of all necessities in early childhood.

God too has provided everything for us. None of us were born with oxygen cylinders! She forgives all our faults just like the Lord. It is said 'God gives and forgives, we get and forget'. She is our first Guru. We must see God in our mother. Then we will also be able to see God in everyone.

पितृदेवो भव

pitṛ devo bhava:

Regard father as God.

He works all day to provide for us and enrich our lives. He may appear to be a hard disciplinarian on the outside but inside he is tender and has love for us.

आचार्य देवो भव ācārya devo bhava:

Regard the teacher as God.

Before we can respect the teacher there must be a desire to learn and respect for knowledge. A student is called vidyārthī. Artha means wealth. Vidyārthī is the one for whom knowledge itself is wealth. Arthī also means 'one desirous of'. Vidyārthī is one desirous of knowledge. When one wants to learn one must be prepared to give up comforts and pleasure.

In the olden days, even princes went to the gurukula (residential school) where all were treated equally. They gave up comforts and served the ācārya (teacher) and brought bhikṣā (food) for him. The students now-a-days study with the radio on, sprawled on the bed. No creative learning can come that way. So we must respect knowledge and the teacher who imparts it.

Next is respect for books. If the book is torn, the cover torn, scribbling all over, the book is thrown about, it shows disrespect. When knowledge is regarded as sacred, there will be great reverence for the books as well as the teacher, who gives us this knowledge.

When a student is eager to learn, he can learn from anyone. There is a story in the Purāṇās of Avadhūta Bhagavān who learned from space, wind, water, the sun, the moon and even from a snake. What is required of us is to tune our mind to the teacher.

अतिथि देवो भव atithi devo bhava

Regard guest as God.

Always pay respect to those who come home and be ever ready to serve them with love. Don't we like to be welcomed warmly when we visit our friends and relatives? We too should do so.

PREPARING FOR THE GAME

In life, preparation for anything takes a long time. To eat food takes fifteen minutes but to prepare it takes months. It starts when seeds are sown, then crops harvested, grains marketed, bought and then the final preparation of cooking may take two hours. So the preparation for the game of life is also a long one. In fact we have to continuously prepare and be prepared at all times to play it well.

What do we do to prepare? It is the mind that needs to be prepared. A well-tuned mind can play well.

How should we tune our mind?

When we want to hear a music program on the radio, we have to tune the radio to the right station. If the radio is tuned to a different wave length, there will be some noise but no music. Similarly when the teacher is speaking, if the student's mind is tuned in to the teacher, then he will understand exactly what the teacher has said. A teacher was demonstrating in the class, "Here are five oranges. Now I have given away three". He asked one boy, "How many remain?" The boy replied, "A tail", because at that time he was watching a mouse disappear into a hole! A teacher told the class, "Pay attention". One boy said, "Yes teacher. I am paying as little as possible". Such children can never learn.

In the earlier days both the teacher and the students together used to chant a prayer before starting studies in order to tune their minds to each other.

ॐ सहनाववतु। सह नौ भुनक्तु।
सह वीर्यं करवावहै।
तेजस्विनावधीतमस्तु मा विद्विषावहै।।
ॐ शान्ति: शान्ति: शान्ति:।।
oṁ sahanāvavatu, saha nau bhunaktu,
saha vīryaṁ karavāvahai,
tejasvināvadhītamastu mā vidviṣāvahai.
Oṁ śāntiḥ śāntiḥ śāntiḥ.

ॐ सहनाववतु। oṁ sahanāvavatu

May the Lord protect us.

Both the teacher and the students pray for the safety and welfare of each other, so that there is no obstruction to learning. The students do not wish that the teacher may fall ill so that they may get a holiday.

सह नौ भुनक्तु saha nau bhunaktu

May we enjoy the fruit of knowledge.

May there be food for thought, not thought of food at the time of learning. Learning and teaching must become joyous to both the student and the teacher.

सह वीर्यं करवावहै saha vīryaṁ karavāvahai

May we put forth the right efforts for learning.

23

The teacher prepares the lessons and attempts as best as he can to explain with patience till the student understands. The student must also put forth efforts to understand, pay attention and revise the previous lessons.

तेजस्विनावधीतमस्तु tejasvināvadhītam-astu

May our intellect be bright.

Bright means the right knowledge comes to us at the right time, not that the knowledge remains in the books.

मा विद्विषावहै mā vidviṣāvahai

May we not dislike each other.

If there is dislike between the teacher and the students, then learning becomes difficult. If the students dislike the teacher, they will throw arrows or talk ill of him and not learn anything. The students should look at the teacher as God and the teacher should look at the students as his own children.

A human being in comparison to animals, has many specialities. One of them is speech. We can speak words and different languages to communicate. If we make proper use of our ability to speak, we can make friends and wealth. Words can save our life or somebody's life. If not used well, we can create enemies. Unintelligent and indiscriminate use of words can invite death also. Speech is a powerful means to express and communicate. It can inspire us, protect us or destroy us. Word power (śabda śakti) is far greater than weapon power (śastra śakti). If it is not properly used, it creates misunderstanding and confusion. That is why it is said:

लक्ष्मीर्वसति जिह्वाग्रे
    जिह्वाग्रे मित्रबान्धवा:
बन्धनं चैव जिह्वाग्रे
    जिह्वाग्रे मरणं ध्रुवम्

lakṣmīr-vasati jihvāgre
    jihvāgre mitrabāndhavāḥ,
bandhanaṁ caiva jihvāgre
    jihvāgre maraṇaṁ dhruvam.

On the tip of the tongue dwells Goddess Lakshmi. On the tip of the tongue are friends and relatives. By words alone one can become bound. By words you can also invite death.

Thus through proper and right usage of words we can earn money, friendship, relations, immortality or death. Pūjya Gurudev was once asked how he got money to run Chinmaya Mission, such a big world-wide institution. He answered, "Because of my ancestral property, three inches of land – my tongue!" That is, by his power of speech. He spoke with great love, devotion, sincerity and imparted knowledge with true feelings. People came in thousands and they brought everything else.

Another thing in life is to know how to speak, how much to speak and with whom to speak.

अविचार्यं न वक्तव्यं
वक्तव्यं सुविचारितम्
किञ्च तत्रैव वक्तव्यं
यत्रोक्तं सफलं भवेत्:

avicāryaṁ na vaktavyaṁ
vaktavyaṁ suvicāritam,
kiñca tatraiva vaktavyaṁ
yatroktaṁ saphalaṁ bhavet.

Do not speak without thinking. Think well before speaking. Speak only if you find it will be fruitful.

Think about the consequences and then speak. Hanumānji never used to speak anything without thinking or even do anything without thinking. 'Will it be good for me and others?' If so speak. 'Will it harm me and others?' If so, don't speak. Never give advice to a person who is not willing to listen. Never speak if others feel it will be interference. Always speak in a pleasant manner since all beings feel happy when they hear pleasant words. Not just men, but animals grow better and plants bloom better when pleasant words are spoken to them. No one likes to hear harsh words, even if it is the truth. Speak the truth or point out mistakes or wrongs in a pleasant and gentle way.

Nothing in this world is accomplished without effort. Physical effort is a must if you want to achieve anything in this world. Results will come only after required effort is put. Success cannot be attained without work. Only in one place – a dictionary – can success be found before work! Everything is accomplished by hard work alone. No amount of imagining and day dreaming will help. Even ordinary actions like eating cannot be accomplished without effort. You cannot sit in front of a plate of laddūs (an Indian sweet) keep your mouth open and expect the laddū to jump in your mouth. Also never postpone anything for tomorrow. Don't wait. Do it today and now. We don't know what will happen in future. Be prepared for the future, but do not worry about the future. In the beginning itself we must think about what can happen and prepare ourselves. Prepare today for a better tomorrow. We don't start digging a well after the house has caught fire. We keep fire extinguishers ready, when the house is built. Such a person is an intelligent person.

In life, if we want to be happy, we should not be dependent on many things. We must learn to be independent. Learn to stand on your own feet and not live on the efforts of your father, brother or father-in-law.

So, in life we must think properly, speak good words, work hard and learn to be independent.

THE ＡCTUAL GAME

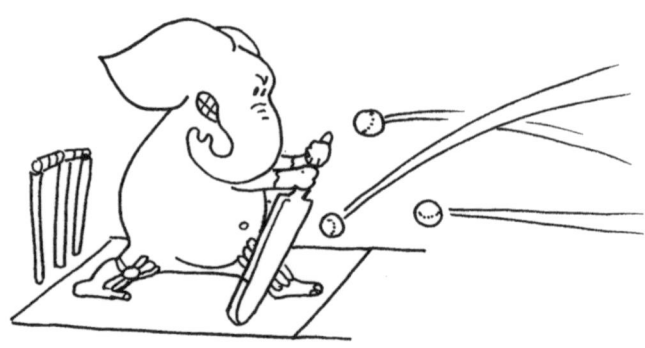

The game of life

Let us take the example of cricket. It is the most popular game in India. In cricket, there is a huge field with the pitch in the centre. There are three stumps on either side. There is a single batsman who has to face the bowler. There are other fielders, all of them trying to get the batsman out. The bowler bowls different kinds of balls and the fielding goes on changing. In the stadium there are thousands of spectators, some who encourage and others who are hostile.

Under such circumstances, how can the batsman be successful?

a.   He must be fearless, not get scared of the bowler, the fielders or the audience.

b.   He must know how to face all types of balls – fast, spin, etc. If he knows how to face only one type of ball, say a fast one, then when a spin is bowled, he gets out.

c.   He must be alert all the time; otherwise he can get clean bowled, run out and so on.

d.   He must maintain his balance and not get excited especially when he is in nineties. If he gets excited and anxious, he gets out.

e.   He must learn to face a hostile crowd with courage and not get overpowered by the tactics of the opposite team. When other members of his team get out, he should not get dejected or over-whelmed by the responsibility to perform well. If he starts hitting, the game livens up again.

f.   His behavior must be good, because all the spectators in the stadium are watching. People are watching on television, listening to the commentary on radio or will read about the game in the newspapers the next day. One man is playing and eyes of the entire nation are on him. In foreign tours especially one act of misbehavior brings bad name not only to the player but to the entire nation. He should not allow the other team to overpower him, in any manner, especially emotionally. This is important.

We now apply this to our life. Our field may be very limited – our house, our school or office. In whichever field we may be working, there are many people who are trying to pull us down. Many people – friends, relatives, and family members encourage us. It is a test.

We face different kinds of bowling – various types of problems – medical problems, family problems, social problems, political problems and so on. If we know how to face only one type of problem, we can solve the problem in that field, but when faced with other problems, we don't know what to do. Hence whether it is loss of health, wealth or emotional disturbance, one must know how to face these problems.

We have to face the challenges from the world with the bat of knowledge and right understanding. We usually have only a college degree, which is inadequate. We need both, knowledge and right understanding. Some have knowledge but no understanding (viveka). So we do not know how to use and where to use that knowledge. Three friends went abroad for higher studies and met after five years. The first one learnt, how to put a dead body together, the second one learnt to give life to the dead body. The third had general understanding about life. They came across a dead tiger cut up by the hunter into pieces. The first one put the pieces together and asked the second to give it life. The third friend cautioned them against it. He went up a tree when they refused to listen to him. The second one gave life to the tiger, which then killed the two friends. Their own knowledge killed them as they had no understanding of how to use it, even after being advised by the third friend.

So discrimination is important but indeed rare to find. Swāmī Vivekānanda observed "The most uncommon thing in the world is common sense". Therefore, we find that only getting degrees does not help us in life. We must understand how to face different situations, what to do in each situation and make the best of it. Bhagavān Śrī Kṛṣṇa had to face many difficult situations but he faced them all with a smile and knew exactly what to do each time.

The three stumps are the body, mind and intellect. When there is a difficult situation or problem, if you become physically weak, emotionally upset and intellectually confused, you cannot find any solution. All the three stumps are down; we get out and have to walk back to the pavilion. So in the game of life, we must stand in the field fearlessly, bat with right discrimination and protect our physical, mental and intellectual stumps from the problems which can shatter them.

Even if we get out quickly, doesn't matter. Play well in the next innings. Never be worried and anxious, otherwise next time also we will fail. Do not take anything for granted. We must be ever alert, just like the soldiers in the army who remain ever alert – even during peace-time.

We must remember that others are watching. We must behave properly and be disciplined during the whole day. A batsman may play only for 5-6 hours but people will watch his behavior all the time. He will be considered great, when he is good all the time.

We may not appreciate all these things at once. Only when we live our life, we will understand slowly, all the rules, laws and dharma that help to develop our personality.

A $\mathcal{G}$REAT GAME

A Great Game

Limited knowledge or a partial knowledge will not help us in facing all kinds of problems or situations that come to us. In our professional life we may be experts in one field. We need not have knowledge of each subject. We need not become doctors, lawyers, engineers, politicians – all in one. We cannot become all that anyway. Specialists are there to treat specific problems. But in order to live our life, we must have a general understanding of total life so that we are prepared to face it and don't become excited or anxious. We generally take one aspect of life as the whole life. This kind of understanding is wrong. We must not give undue importance to one part or aspect and neglect the others. We need to have a complete understanding of the whole picture of life. We will not be able to refer to books all the time. We must ourselves know about life and play the game of life. If we take it lightly then life can become terrible. If we take it seriously and understand it completely, then life becomes fun.

When playing the game there are situations when both the teams have a conflict and they have to surrender to somebody for a decision – to the umpire. Both teams must have full faith in him, otherwise the decision is not accepted. In life also, the supreme umpire is God. We must have full faith in Him and surrender to His decisions. There may be many seen umpires – mother, father, teacher – who advise us and guide us when we are in difficult situations. Lakṣmaṇa did not agree with Śrī Rāma on many occasions, but he accepted anything Śrī Rāma said. Arjuna wanted to run away from the battlefield but he asked Lord Kṛṣṇa what to do. That was the best thing he did. Śrī Kṛṣṇa gave him good advice and he followed it, so he won the war.

Many times it so happens that events occur and then we feel we have been cheated. In examinations we feel we have written everything correctly, yet we get low marks. There is a tendency to feel that we are cent percent right and others are wrong.

Swāmī Rāma Tīrthajī once said, "In life we get what we deserve and not what we desire". Have full faith that we get what we deserve and that the Lord is not partial. He shows no favoritism. Let us deserve to get what we desire, and then we will get it. What comes to us is quite proper and just. Have faith, that whatever happens is the right thing. Then whatever happens, I gain from it. I may not immediately understand the gain. We have to learn from various experiences. We must have faith in the justice and the goodness of God.

After pūjā, whatever is distributed as prasāda, we take it without complaints. Whether it is big or small, whether it is a flower, fruit, coconut, candana or vibhūtī; we accept it with gratitude and reverence. Prasāda means prasannatā (cheerful acceptance). In life also whatever I get, it is coming from the Lord, so accept it cheerfully. I accept it whether I consider it good or bad. Even if my leg breaks it is Bhagavān's prasāda. Have faith that the entire nature is governed by the Lord. **You do your best and then accept what comes as His prasāda.**

Thus play the game of life. Life is yours. You have no choice but to live it. There is no running away. Play it with true sportsman spirit so that ultimately you succeed. Live life in such a way that you enjoy and other people derive inspiration from you in living their lives. Then there is joy and joy alone. Such is a great game and a great player.

Om tat sat

□□□